FOLLOWING JESUS JOURNAL

a one year Bible
reading plan

ISBN 978-1-64744-165-4

Published by Outreach, Inc. Colorado Springs, CO 80919
www.Outreach.com

Interior Design by Alexia Garaventa

HOW TO USE THE FOLLOWING JESUS JOURNAL

"All Scripture is God-breathed and is useful for teaching, rebuking, correcting and training in righteousness."

2 Timothy 3:16 NIV

Our journey in *Following Jesus* begins from the moment we confess that Jesus is Lord (Romans 10:9-10). At that moment we are saved from the consequences of our sin and brought close to God again. And while our salvation is instant, the process of God maturing and purifying us is a daily process. The Bible says, "Being confident of this, that he who began a good work in you will carry it on to completion until the DAY of Christ Jesus" (Philippians 1:6 NIV). God is inviting us into an ongoing daily rhythm of relationship and development. He didn't just save you to leave you on your own; He is a good heavenly Father who is interested in knowing you personally and shaping, equipping, and releasing you into your purpose. We engage with the Bible daily because the Word of God is life, light, strength, hope, and power. The Bible calls the Word the Bread of Life! We need a daily intake of life to keep us alive and thriving.

The reason we created this journal is to help you with the simple but essential discipline of the Christian faith, which is to learn to hear from God personally and to obey God's Word by putting it into practice. As you read the Bible and use the SOAP Bible study and journaling strategy, you'll see your life being transformed daily! Going to God's Word with the expectation that He is going to speak to you as well as engaging in the discipline of applying God's Word will transform every area of your life. Going to church and hearing solid preaching from your pastor is very important, but that doesn't replace your need to hear from the Holy Spirit on a daily basis. Before you start your devotional time, ask the Holy Spirit to speak to you as you read His Word. Watch how God's Word will come alive in your life. As you know and follow it, the Bible will transform your life and the world around you!

EFFECTIVE BIBLE READING

To help you maximize your Bible reading, we encourage you to use a daily Bible reading plan in partnership with the SOAP Bible study and journaling approach. We created a 365-DAY *Following Jesus* reading plan that this journal uses. It is also available digitally on the YouVersion Bible app. As you read daily, use the SOAP acronym to help you apply God's Word to your life.

S = SCRIPTURE

As you're reading, look for one verse that really sticks out to you. When a verse jumps out, circle the verse number or highlight it on your phone so you can go back to it later. After you're done reading all the chapters, write out the one verse that you want to focus on at the top of your journal page.

O = OBSERVATION

Now it's time to take a few moments to write down your observations about that specific verse. What do you see? What do you feel God saying to you about it? What seems to be the point of the verse?

A = APPLICATION

Write down how you're going to apply this verse to your life. What action will you take? Ask yourself each DAY, "How will I be different toDAY after reading this verse?"

P = PRAYER

Write out a prayer to God for the DAY in connection with the verse you've just been reading and meditating on. Note: Some DAYs will have more specific application after reading than other DAYs; don't worry about that. Some DAYs might cover things you're already doing, and other DAYs you'll have a lot to work on.

*We adapted the SOAP journaling plan from Wayne Cordeiro.

FOLLOWING JESUS BIBLE READING PLAN

For your daily reading, you can use the plan in this journal and check off the DAYs as you complete them, or you can scan and download the *Following Jesus* app and find the one-year plan on the YouVersion Bible app. The *Following Jesus* one-year Bible reading plan will take you through the whole Old Testament once, repeating the book of Psalms and the book of Proverbs multiple times in the year. It will also take you through the whole New Testament once, with a few selections read twice.

- ☐ DAY 1: Genesis 1, Genesis 2, Psalm 1, Matthew 1
- ☐ DAY 2: Genesis 3, Genesis 4, Psalm 2, Matthew 2
- ☐ DAY 3: Genesis 5, Genesis 6, Proverbs 1, Matthew 3
- ☐ DAY 4: Genesis 7, Genesis 8, Proverbs 2, Matthew 4
- ☐ DAY 5: Genesis 9, Genesis 10, Psalm 3, Matthew 5
- ☐ DAY 6: Genesis 11, Genesis 12, Psalm 4, Matthew 6
- ☐ DAY 7: Genesis 13, Genesis 14, Proverbs 3, Matthew 7
- ☐ DAY 8: Genesis 15, Genesis 16, Proverbs 4, Matthew 8
- ☐ DAY 9: Genesis 17, Genesis 18, Psalm 5, Matthew 9
- ☐ DAY 10: Genesis 19, Genesis 20, Psalm 6, Matthew 10
- ☐ DAY 11: Genesis 21, Genesis 22, Proverbs 5, Matthew 11
- ☐ DAY 12: Genesis 23, Genesis 24, Proverbs 6, Matthew 12
- ☐ DAY 13: Genesis 25, Genesis 26, Psalm 7, Matthew 13
- ☐ DAY 14: Genesis 27, Genesis 28, Psalm 8, Matthew 14
- ☐ DAY 15: Genesis 29, Genesis 30, Proverbs 7, Matthew 15
- ☐ DAY 16: Genesis 31, Genesis 32, Proverbs 8, Matthew 16
- ☐ DAY 17: Genesis 33, Genesis 34, Psalm 9, Matthew 17
- ☐ DAY 18: Genesis 35, Genesis 36, Psalm 10, Matthew 18
- ☐ DAY 19: Genesis 37, Genesis 38, Genesis 39, Proverbs 9, Matthew 19
- ☐ DAY 20: Genesis 40, Genesis 41, Proverbs 10, Matthew 20
- ☐ DAY 21: Genesis 42, Genesis 43, Psalm 11, Matthew 21
- ☐ DAY 22: Genesis 44, Genesis 45, Psalm 12, Matthew 22
- ☐ DAY 23: Genesis 46, Genesis 47, Proverbs 11, Matthew 23
- ☐ DAY 24: Genesis 48, Genesis 49, Proverbs 12, Matthew 24
- ☐ DAY 25: Genesis 50, Exodus 1, Psalm 13, Matthew 25
- ☐ DAY 26: Exodus 2, Exodus 3, Psalm 14, Matthew 26
- ☐ DAY 27: Exodus 4, Exodus 5, Proverbs 13, Matthew 27
- ☐ DAY 28: Exodus 6, Exodus 7, Proverbs 14, Matthew 28
- ☐ DAY 29: Exodus 8, Exodus 9, Psalm 15, Mark 1
- ☐ DAY 30: Exodus 10, Exodus 11, Psalm 16, Mark 2

- ☐ DAY 31: Exodus 12, Exodus 13, Proverbs 15, Mark 3
- ☐ DAY 32: Exodus 14, Exodus 15, Proverbs 16, Mark 4
- ☐ DAY 33: Exodus 16, Exodus 17, Psalm 17, Mark 5
- ☐ DAY 34: Exodus 18, Exodus 19, Psalm 18, Mark 6
- ☐ DAY 35: Exodus 20, Exodus 21, Proverbs 17, Mark 7
- ☐ DAY 36: Exodus 22, Exodus 23, Proverbs 18, Mark 8
- ☐ DAY 37: Exodus 24, Exodus 25, Psalm 19, Mark 9
- ☐ DAY 38: Exodus 26, Exodus 27, Exodus 28, Psalm 20, Mark 10
- ☐ DAY 39: Exodus 29, Exodus 30, Proverbs 19, Mark 11
- ☐ DAY 40: Exodus 31, Exodus 32, Proverbs 20, Mark 12
- ☐ DAY 41: Exodus 33, Exodus 34, Psalm 21, Mark 13
- ☐ DAY 42: Exodus 35, Exodus 36, Psalm 22, Mark 14
- ☐ DAY 43: Exodus 37, Exodus 38, Proverbs 21, Mark 15
- ☐ DAY 44: Exodus 39, Exodus 40, Proverbs 22, Mark 16
- ☐ DAY 45: Leviticus 1, Leviticus 2, Psalm 23, Luke 1
- ☐ DAY 46: Leviticus 3, Leviticus 4, Psalm 24, Luke 2
- ☐ DAY 47: Leviticus 5, Leviticus 6, Proverbs 23, Luke 3
- ☐ DAY 48: Leviticus 7, Leviticus 8, Proverbs 24, Luke 4
- ☐ DAY 49: Leviticus 9, Leviticus 10, Psalm 25, Luke 5
- ☐ DAY 50: Leviticus 11, Leviticus 12, Psalm 26, Luke 6
- ☐ DAY 51: Leviticus 13, Leviticus 14, Proverbs 25, Luke 7
- ☐ DAY 52: Leviticus 15, Leviticus 16, Proverbs 26, Luke 8
- ☐ DAY 53: Leviticus 17, Leviticus 18, Psalm 27, Luke 9
- ☐ DAY 54: Leviticus 19, Leviticus 20, Psalm 28, Luke 10
- ☐ DAY 55: Leviticus 21, Leviticus 22, Proverbs 27, Luke 11
- ☐ DAY 56: Leviticus 23, Leviticus 24, Proverbs 28, Luke 12
- ☐ DAY 57: Leviticus 25, Leviticus 26, Leviticus 27, Psalm 29, Luke 13
- ☐ DAY 58: Numbers 1, Numbers 2, Psalm 30, Luke 14
- ☐ DAY 59: Numbers 3, Numbers 4, Proverbs 29, Luke 15
- ☐ DAY 60: Numbers 5, Numbers 6, Proverbs 30, Luke 16
- ☐ DAY 61: Numbers 7, Numbers 8, Proverbs 31, Luke 17
- ☐ DAY 62: Numbers 9, Numbers 10, Psalm 31, Luke 18
- ☐ DAY 63: Numbers 11, Numbers 12, Psalm 32, Luke 19
- ☐ DAY 64: Numbers 13, Numbers 14, Proverbs 1, Luke 20
- ☐ DAY 65: Numbers 15, Numbers 16, Proverbs 2, Luke 21
- ☐ DAY 66: Numbers 17, Numbers 18, Psalm 33, Luke 22
- ☐ DAY 67: Numbers 19, Numbers 20, Psalm 34, Luke 23
- ☐ DAY 68: Numbers 21, Numbers 22, Proverbs 3, Luke 24
- ☐ DAY 69: Numbers 23, Numbers 24, Proverbs 4, John 1
- ☐ DAY 70: Numbers 25, Numbers 26, Psalm 35, John 2
- ☐ DAY 71: Numbers 27, Numbers 28, Psalm 36, John 3
- ☐ DAY 72: Numbers 29, Numbers 30, Proverbs 5, John 4
- ☐ DAY 73: Numbers 31, Numbers 32, Proverbs 6, John 5
- ☐ DAY 74: Numbers 33, Numbers 34, Psalm 37, John 6
- ☐ DAY 75: Numbers 35, Numbers 36, Psalm 38, John 7
- ☐ DAY 76: Deuteronomy 1, Deuteronomy 2, Deuteronomy 3, Proverbs 7, John 8
- ☐ DAY 77: Deuteronomy 4, Deuteronomy 5, Proverbs 8, John 9
- ☐ DAY 78: Deuteronomy 6, Deuteronomy 7, Psalm 39, John 10
- ☐ DAY 79: Deuteronomy 8, Deuteronomy 9, Psalm 40, John 11
- ☐ DAY 80: Deuteronomy 10, Deuteronomy 11, Proverbs 9, John 12

- ☐ DAY 81: Deuteronomy 12, Deuteronomy 13, Proverbs 10, John 13
- ☐ DAY 82: Deuteronomy 14, Deuteronomy 15, Psalm 41, John 14
- ☐ DAY 83: Deuteronomy 16, Deuteronomy 17, Psalm 42, John 15
- ☐ DAY 84: Deuteronomy 18, Deuteronomy 19, Proverbs 11, John 16
- ☐ DAY 85: Deuteronomy 20, Deuteronomy 21, Proverbs 12, John 17
- ☐ DAY 86: Deuteronomy 22, Deuteronomy 23, Psalm 43, John 18
- ☐ DAY 87: Deuteronomy 24, Deuteronomy 25, Psalm 44, John 19
- ☐ DAY 88: Deuteronomy 26, Deuteronomy 27, Proverbs 13, John 20
- ☐ DAY 89: Deuteronomy 28, Deuteronomy 29, Proverbs 14, John 21
- ☐ DAY 90: Deuteronomy 30, Deuteronomy 31, Psalm 45, Acts 1
- ☐ DAY 91: Deuteronomy 32, Deuteronomy 33, Psalm 46, Acts 2
- ☐ DAY 92: Deuteronomy 34, Joshua 1, Proverbs 15, Acts 3
- ☐ DAY 93: Joshua 2, Joshua 3, Proverbs 16, Acts 4
- ☐ DAY 94: Joshua 4, Joshua 5, Psalm 47, Acts 5
- ☐ DAY 95: Joshua 6, Joshua 7, Joshua 8, Psalm 48, Acts 6
- ☐ DAY 96: Joshua 9, Joshua 10, Proverbs 17, Acts 7
- ☐ DAY 97: Joshua 11, Joshua 12, Proverbs 18, Acts 8
- ☐ DAY 98: Joshua 13, Joshua 14, Psalm 49, Acts 9
- ☐ DAY 99: Joshua 15, Joshua 16, Psalm 50, Acts 10
- ☐ DAY 100: Joshua 17, Joshua 18, Proverbs 19, Acts 11
- ☐ DAY 101: Joshua 19, Joshua 20, Proverbs 20, Acts 12
- ☐ DAY 102: Joshua 21, Joshua 22, Psalm 51, Acts 13
- ☐ DAY 103: Joshua 23, Joshua 24, Psalm 52, Acts 14
- ☐ DAY 104: Judges 1, Judges 2, Proverbs 21, Acts 15
- ☐ DAY 105: Judges 3, Judges 4, Proverbs 22, Acts 16
- ☐ DAY 106: Judges 5, Judges 6, Psalm 53, Acts 17
- ☐ DAY 107: Judges 7, Judges 8, Psalm 54, Acts 18
- ☐ DAY 108: Judges 9, Judges 10, Proverbs 23, Acts 19
- ☐ DAY 109: Judges 11, Judges 12, Proverbs 24, Acts 20
- ☐ DAY 110: Judges 13, Judges 14, Psalm 55, Acts 21
- ☐ DAY 111: Judges 15, Judges 16, Psalm 56, Acts 22
- ☐ DAY 112: Judges 17, Judges 18, Proverbs 25, Acts 23
- ☐ DAY 113: Judges 19, Judges 20, Proverbs 26, Acts 24
- ☐ DAY 114: Judges 21, Ruth 1, Ruth 2, Psalm 57, Acts 25
- ☐ DAY 115: Ruth 3, Ruth 4, Psalm 58, Acts 26
- ☐ DAY 116: 1 Samuel 1, 1 Samuel 2, Proverbs 27, Acts 27
- ☐ DAY 117: 1 Samuel 3, 1 Samuel 4, Proverbs 28, Acts 28
- ☐ DAY 118: 1 Samuel 5, 1 Samuel 6, Psalm 59, Romans 1
- ☐ DAY 119: 1 Samuel 7, 1 Samuel 8, Psalm 60, Romans 2
- ☐ DAY 120: 1 Samuel 9, 1 Samuel 10, Proverbs 29, Romans 3
- ☐ DAY 121: 1 Samuel 11, 1 Samuel 12, Proverbs 30, Romans 4
- ☐ DAY 122: 1 Samuel 13, 1 Samuel 14, Proverbs 31, Romans 5
- ☐ DAY 123: 1 Samuel 15, 1 Samuel 16, Psalm 61, Romans 6
- ☐ DAY 124: 1 Samuel 17, 1 Samuel 18, Psalm 62, Romans 7
- ☐ DAY 125: 1 Samuel 19, 1 Samuel 20, Proverbs 1, Romans 8
- ☐ DAY 126: 1 Samuel 21, 1 Samuel 22, Proverbs 2, Romans 9
- ☐ DAY 127: 1 Samuel 23, 1 Samuel 24, Psalm 63, Romans 10
- ☐ DAY 128: 1 Samuel 25, 1 Samuel 26, Psalm 64, Romans 11
- ☐ DAY 129: 1 Samuel 27, 1 Samuel 28, Proverbs 3, Romans 12
- ☐ DAY 130: 1 Samuel 29, 1 Samuel 30, Proverbs 4, Romans 13

☐ DAY 131: 1 Samuel 31, 2 Samuel 1, Psalm 65, Romans 14

☐ DAY 132: 2 Samuel 2, 2 Samuel 3, Psalm 66, Romans 15

☐ DAY 133: 2 Samuel 4, 2 Samuel 5, 2 Samuel 6, Proverbs 5, Romans 16

☐ DAY 134: 2 Samuel 7, 2 Samuel 8, Proverbs 6, 1 Corinthians 1

☐ DAY 135: 2 Samuel 9, 2 Samuel 10, Psalm 67, 1 Corinthians 2

☐ DAY 136: 2 Samuel 11, 2 Samuel 12, Psalm 68, 1 Corinthians 3

☐ DAY 137: 2 Samuel 13, 2 Samuel 14, Proverbs 7, 1 Corinthians 4

☐ DAY 138: 2 Samuel 15, 2 Samuel 16, Proverbs 8, 1 Corinthians 5

☐ DAY 139: 2 Samuel 17, 2 Samuel 18, Psalm 69, 1 Corinthians 6

☐ DAY 140: 2 Samuel 19, 2 Samuel 20, Psalm 70, 1 Corinthians 7

☐ DAY 141: 2 Samuel 21, 2 Samuel 22, Proverbs 9, 1 Corinthians 8

☐ DAY 142: 2 Samuel 23, 2 Samuel 24, Proverbs 10, 1 Corinthians 9

☐ DAY 143: 1 Kings 1, 1 Kings 2, Psalm 71, 1 Corinthians 10

☐ DAY 144: 1 Kings 3, 1 Kings 4, Psalm 72, 1 Corinthians 11

☐ DAY 145: 1 Kings 5, 1 Kings 6, Proverbs 11, 1 Corinthians 12

☐ DAY 146: 1 Kings 7, 1 Kings 8, Proverbs 12, 1 Corinthians 13

☐ DAY 147: 1 Kings 9, 1 Kings 10, Psalm 73, 1 Corinthians 14

☐ DAY 148: 1 Kings 11, 1 Kings 12, Psalm 74, 1 Corinthians 15

☐ DAY 149: 1 Kings 13, 1 Kings 14, Proverbs 13, 1 Corinthians 16

☐ DAY 150: 1 Kings 15, 1 Kings 16, Proverbs 14, 2 Corinthians 1

☐ DAY 151: 1 Kings 17, 1 Kings 18, Psalm 75, 2 Corinthians 2

☐ DAY 152: 1 Kings 19, 1 Kings 20, 1 Kings 21, Psalm 76, 2 Corinthians 3

☐ DAY 153: 1 Kings 22, 2 Kings 1, Proverbs 15, 2 Corinthians 4

☐ DAY 154: 2 Kings 2, 2 Kings 3, Proverbs 16, 2 Corinthians 5

☐ DAY 155: 2 Kings 4, 2 Kings 5, Psalm 77, 2 Corinthians 6

☐ DAY 156: 2 Kings 6, 2 Kings 7, Psalm 78, 2 Corinthians 7

☐ DAY 157: 2 Kings 8, 2 Kings 9, Proverbs 17, 2 Corinthians 8

☐ DAY 158: 2 Kings 10, 2 Kings 11, Proverbs 18, 2 Corinthians 9

☐ DAY 159: 2 Kings 12, 2 Kings 13, Psalm 79, 2 Corinthians 10

☐ DAY 160: 2 Kings 14, 2 Kings 15, Psalm 80, 2 Corinthians 11

☐ DAY 161: 2 Kings 16, 2 Kings 17, Proverbs 19, 2 Corinthians 12

☐ DAY 162: 2 Kings 18, 2 Kings 19, Proverbs 20, 2 Corinthians 13

☐ DAY 163: 2 Kings 20, 2 Kings 21, Psalm 81, Galatians 1

☐ DAY 164: 2 Kings 22, 2 Kings 23, Psalm 82, Galatians 2

☐ DAY 165: 2 Kings 24, 2 Kings 25, Proverbs 21, Galatians 3

☐ DAY 166: 1 Chronicles 1, 1 Chronicles 2, Proverbs 22, Galatians 4

☐ DAY 167: 1 Chronicles 3, 1 Chronicles 4, Psalm 83, Galatians 5

☐ DAY 168: 1 Chronicles 5, 1 Chronicles 6, Psalm 84, Galatians 6

☐ DAY 169: 1 Chronicles 7, 1 Chronicles 8, Proverbs 23, Ephesians 1

☐ DAY 170: 1 Chronicles 9, 1 Chronicles 10, Proverbs 24, Ephesians 2

☐ DAY 171: 1 Chronicles 11, 1 Chronicles 12, 1 Chronicles 13, Psalm 85, Ephesians 3

☐ DAY 172: 1 Chronicles 14, 1 Chronicles 15, Psalm 86, Ephesians 4

☐ DAY 173: 1 Chronicles 16, 1 Chronicles 17, Proverbs 25, Ephesians 5

☐ DAY 174: 1 Chronicles 18, 1 Chronicles 19, Proverbs 26, Ephesians 6

☐ DAY 175: 1 Chronicles 20, 1 Chronicles 21, Psalm 87, Philippians 1

☐ DAY 176:1 Chronicles 22, 1 Chronicles 23, Psalm 88, Philippians 2

☐ DAY 177: 1 Chronicles 24, 1 Chronicles 25, Proverbs 27, Philippians 3

☐ DAY 178: 1 Chronicles 26, 1 Chronicles 27, Proverbs 28, Philippians 4

☐ DAY 179: 1 Chronicles 28, 1 Chronicles 29, Psalm 89, Colossians 1

☐ DAY 180: 2 Chronicles 1, 2 Chronicles 2, Psalm 90, Colossians 2

☐ DAY 181: 2 Chronicles 3, 2 Chronicles 4, Proverbs 29, Colossians 3

☐ DAY 182: 2 Chronicles 5, 2 Chronicles 6, Proverbs 30, Colossians 4

☐ DAY 183: 2 Chronicles 7, 2 Chronicles 8, Proverbs 31, 1 Thessalonians 1

☐ DAY 184: 2 Chronicles 9, 2 Chronicles 10, Psalm 91, 1 Thessalonians 2

☐ DAY 185: 2 Chronicles 11, 2 Chronicles 12, Psalm 92, 1 Thessalonians 3

☐ DAY 186: 2 Chronicles 13, 2 Chronicles 14, Proverbs 1, 1 Thessalonians 4

☐ DAY 187: 2 Chronicles 15, 2 Chronicles 16, Proverbs 2, 1 Thessalonians 5

☐ DAY 188: 2 Chronicles 17, 2 Chronicles 18, Psalm 93, 2 Thessalonians 1

☐ DAY 189: 2 Chronicles 19, 2 Chronicles 20, Psalm 94, 2 Thessalonians 2

☐ DAY 190: 2 Chronicles 21, 2 Chronicles 22, 2 Chronicles 23, Proverbs 3, 2 Thessalonians 3

☐ DAY 191: 2 Chronicles 24, 2 Chronicles 25, Proverbs 4, 1 Timothy 1

☐ DAY 192: 2 Chronicles 26, 2 Chronicles 27, Psalm 95, 1 Timothy 2

☐ DAY 193: 2 Chronicles 28, 2 Chronicles 29, Psalm 96, 1 Timothy 3

☐ DAY 194: 2 Chronicles 30, 2 Chronicles 31, Proverbs 5, 1 Timothy 4

☐ DAY 195: 2 Chronicles 32, 2 Chronicles 33, Proverbs 6, 1 Timothy 5

☐ DAY 196: 2 Chronicles 34, 2 Chronicles 35, Psalm 97, 1 Timothy 6

☐ DAY 197: 2 Chronicles 36, Ezra 1, Psalm 98, 2 Timothy 1

☐ DAY 198: Ezra 2, Ezra 3, Proverbs 7, 2 Timothy 2

☐ DAY 199: Ezra 4, Ezra 5, Proverbs 8, 2 Timothy 3

☐ DAY 200: Ezra 6, Ezra 7, Psalm 99, 2 Timothy 4

☐ DAY 201: Ezra 8, Ezra 9, Psalm 100, Titus 1

☐ DAY 202: Ezra 10, Nehemiah 1, Proverbs 9, Titus 2

☐ DAY 203: Nehemiah 2, Nehemiah 3, Proverbs 10, Titus 3

☐ DAY 204: Nehemiah 4, Nehemiah 5, Psalm 101, Philemon 1

☐ DAY 205: Nehemiah 6, Nehemiah 7, Psalm 102, Hebrews 1

☐ DAY 206: Nehemiah 8, Nehemiah 9, Proverbs 11, Hebrews 2

☐ DAY 207: Nehemiah 10, Nehemiah 11, Proverbs 12, Hebrews 3

☐ DAY 208: Nehemiah 12, Nehemiah 13, Psalm 103, Hebrews 4

☐ DAY 209: Esther 1, Esther 2, Esther 3, Psalm 104, Hebrews 5

☐ DAY 210: Esther 4, Esther 5, Proverbs 13, Hebrews 6

☐ DAY 211: Esther 6, Esther 7, Proverbs 14, Hebrews 7

☐ DAY 212: Esther 8, Esther 9, Psalm 105, Hebrews 8

☐ DAY 213: Esther 10, Job 1, Psalm 106, Hebrews 9

☐ DAY 214: Job 2, Job 3, Proverbs 15, Hebrews 10

☐ DAY 215: Job 4, Job 5, Proverbs 16, Hebrews 11

☐ DAY 216: Job 6, Job 7, Psalm 107, Hebrews 12

☐ DAY 217: Job 8, Job 9, Psalm 108, Hebrews 13

☐ DAY 218: Job 10, Job 11, Proverbs 17, James 1

☐ DAY 219: Job 12, Job 13, Proverbs 18, James 2

☐ DAY 220: Job 14, Job 15, Psalm 109, James 3

☐ DAY 221: Job 16, Job 17, Psalm 110, James 4

☐ DAY 222: Job 18, Job 19, Proverbs 19, James 5

☐ DAY 223: Job 20, Job 21, Proverbs 20, 1 Peter 1

☐ DAY 224: Job 22, Job 23, Psalm 111, 1 Peter 2

☐ DAY 225: Job 24, Job 25, Psalm 112, 1 Peter 3

☐ DAY 226: Job 26, Job 27, Proverbs 21, 1 Peter 4

☐ DAY 227: Job 28, Job 29, Proverbs 22, 1 Peter 5

☐ DAY 228: Job 30, Job 31, Job 32, Psalm 113, 2 Peter 1

☐ DAY 229: Job 33, Job 34, Psalm 114, 2 Peter 2

☐ DAY 230: Job 35, Job 36, Proverbs 23, 2 Peter 3

☐ DAY 231: Job 37, Job 38, Proverbs 24, 1 John 1

☐ DAY 232: Job 39, Job 40, Psalm 115, 1 John 2

☐ DAY 233: Job 41, Job 42, Psalm 116, 1 John 3

☐ DAY 234: Ecclesiastes 1, Ecclesiastes 2, Proverbs 25, 1 John 4

☐ DAY 235: Ecclesiastes 3, Ecclesiastes 4, Proverbs 26, 1 John 5

☐ DAY 236: Ecclesiastes 5, Ecclesiastes 6, Psalm 117, 2 John 1

☐ DAY 237: Ecclesiastes 7, Ecclesiastes 8, Psalm 118, 3 John 1

☐ DAY 238: Ecclesiastes 9, Ecclesiastes 10, Proverbs 27, Jude 1

☐ DAY 239: Ecclesiastes 11, Ecclesiastes 12, Proverbs 28, Revelation 1

☐ DAY 240: Song of Songs 1, Song of Songs 2, Psalm 119:1-16, Revelation 2

☐ DAY 241: Song of Songs 3, Song of Songs 4, Psalm 119:17-32, Revelation 3

☐ DAY 242: Song of Songs 5, Song of Songs 6, Proverbs 29, Revelation 4

☐ DAY 243: Song of Songs 7, Song of Songs 8, Proverbs 30, Revelation 5

☐ DAY 244: Isaiah 1, Isaiah 2, Proverbs 31, Revelation 6

☐ DAY 245: Isaiah 3, Isaiah 4, Psalm 119:33-48, Revelation 7

☐ DAY 246: Isaiah 5, Isaiah 6, Psalm 119:49-64, Revelation 8

☐ DAY 247: Isaiah 7, Isaiah 8, Isaiah 9, Proverbs 1, Revelation 9

☐ DAY 248: Isaiah 10, Isaiah 11, Proverbs 2, Revelation 10

☐ DAY 249: Isaiah 12, Isaiah 13, Psalm 119:65-80, Revelation 11

☐ DAY 250: Isaiah 14, Isaiah 15, Psalm 119:81-96, Revelation 12

☐ DAY 251: Isaiah 16, Isaiah 17, Proverbs 3, Revelation 13

☐ DAY 252: Isaiah 18, Isaiah 19, Proverbs 4, Revelation 14

☐ DAY 253: Isaiah 20, Isaiah 21, Psalm 119:97-112, Revelation 15

☐ DAY 254: Isaiah 22, Isaiah 23, Psalm 119:113-128, Revelation 16

☐ DAY 255: Isaiah 24, Isaiah 25, Proverbs 5, Revelation 17

☐ DAY 256: Isaiah 26, Isaiah 27, Proverbs 6, Revelation 18

☐ DAY 257: Isaiah 28, Isaiah 29, Psalm 119:129-144, Revelation 19

☐ DAY 258: Isaiah 30, Isaiah 31, Psalm 119:145-160, Revelation 20

☐ DAY 259: Isaiah 32, Isaiah 33, Proverbs 7, Revelation 21

☐ DAY 260: Isaiah 34, Isaiah 35, Proverbs 8, Revelation 22

☐ DAY 261: Isaiah 36, Isaiah 37, Psalm 119:161-176, Matthew 1

☐ DAY 262: Isaiah 38, Isaiah 39, Psalm 120, Matthew 2

☐ DAY 263: Isaiah 40, Isaiah 41, Proverbs 9, Matthew 3

☐ DAY 264: Isaiah 42, Isaiah 43, Proverbs 10, Matthew 4

☐ DAY 265: Isaiah 44, Isaiah 45, Psalm 121, Matthew 5

☐ DAY 266: Isaiah 46, Isaiah 47, Isaiah 48, Psalm 122, Matthew 6

☐ DAY 267: Isaiah 49, Isaiah 50, Proverbs 11, Matthew 7

☐ DAY 268: Isaiah 51, Isaiah 52, Proverbs 12, Matthew 8

☐ DAY 269: Isaiah 53, Isaiah 54, Psalm 123, Matthew 9

☐ DAY 270: Isaiah 55, Isaiah 56, Psalm 124, Matthew 10

☐ DAY 271: Isaiah 57, Isaiah 58, Proverbs 13, Matthew 11

☐ DAY 272: Isaiah 59, Isaiah 60, Proverbs 14, Matthew 12

☐ DAY 273: Isaiah 61, Isaiah 62, Psalm 125, Matthew 13

☐ DAY 274: Isaiah 63, Isaiah 64, Psalm 126, Matthew 14

☐ DAY 275: Isaiah 65, Isaiah 66, Proverbs 15, Matthew 15

☐ DAY 276: Jeremiah 1, Jeremiah 2, Proverbs 16, Matthew 16

☐ DAY 277: Jeremiah 3, Jeremiah 4, Psalm 127, Matthew 17

☐ DAY 278: Jeremiah 5, Jeremiah 6, Psalm 128, Matthew 18

☐ DAY 279: Jeremiah 7, Jeremiah 8, Proverbs 17, Matthew 19

☐ DAY 280: Jeremiah 9, Jeremiah 10, Proverbs 18, Matthew 20

☐ DAY 281: Jeremiah 11, Jeremiah 12, Psalm 129, Matthew 21

☐ DAY 282: Jeremiah 13, Jeremiah 14, Psalm 130, Matthew 22

☐ DAY 283: Jeremiah 15, Jeremiah 16, Proverbs 19, Matthew 23

☐ DAY 284: Jeremiah 17, Jeremiah 18, Proverbs 20, Matthew 24

☐ DAY 285: Jeremiah 19, Jeremiah 20, Jeremiah 21, Psalm 131, Matthew 25

☐ DAY 286: Jeremiah 22, Jeremiah 23, Psalm 132, Matthew 26

☐ DAY 287: Jeremiah 24, Jeremiah 25, Proverbs 21, Matthew 27

☐ DAY 288: Jeremiah 26, Jeremiah 27, Proverbs 22, Matthew 28

☐ DAY 289: Jeremiah 28, Jeremiah 29, Psalm 133, Mark 1

☐ DAY 290: Jeremiah 30, Jeremiah 31, Psalm 134, Mark 2

☐ DAY 291: Jeremiah 32, Jeremiah 33, Proverbs 23, Mark 3

☐ DAY 292: Jeremiah 34, Jeremiah 35, Proverbs 24, Mark 4

☐ DAY 293: Jeremiah 36, Jeremiah 37, Psalm 135, Mark 5

☐ DAY 294: Jeremiah 38, Jeremiah 39, Psalm 136, Mark 6

☐ DAY 295: Jeremiah 40, Jeremiah 41, Proverbs 25, Mark 7

☐ DAY 296: Jeremiah 42, Jeremiah 43, Proverbs 26, Mark 8

☐ DAY 297: Jeremiah 44, Jeremiah 45, Psalm 137, Mark 9

☐ DAY 298: Jeremiah 46, Jeremiah 47, Psalm 138, Mark 10

☐ DAY 299: Jeremiah 48, Jeremiah 49, Proverbs 27, Mark 11

☐ DAY 300: Jeremiah 50, Jeremiah 51, Proverbs 28, Mark 12

☐ DAY 301: Jeremiah 52, Lamentations 1, Psalm 139, Mark 13

☐ DAY 302: Lamentations 2, Lamentations 3, Psalm 140, Mark 14

☐ DAY 303: Lamentations 4, Lamentations 5, Proverbs 29, Mark 15

☐ DAY 304: Ezekiel 1, Ezekiel 2, Ezekiel 3, Proverbs 30, Mark 16

☐ DAY 305: Ezekiel 4, Ezekiel 5, Proverbs 31, Luke 1

☐ DAY 306: Ezekiel 6, Ezekiel 7, Psalm 141, Luke 2

☐ DAY 307: Ezekiel 8, Ezekiel 9, Psalm 142, Luke 3

☐ DAY 308: Ezekiel 10, Ezekiel 11, Proverbs 2, Luke 4

☐ DAY 309: Ezekiel 12, Ezekiel 13, Proverbs 3, Luke 5

☐ DAY 310: Ezekiel 14, Ezekiel 15, Psalm 143, Luke 6

☐ DAY 311: Ezekiel 16, Ezekiel 17, Psalm 144, Luke 7

☐ DAY 312: Ezekiel 18, Ezekiel 19, Proverbs 4, Luke 8

☐ DAY 313: Ezekiel 20, Ezekiel 21, Proverbs 5, Luke 9

☐ DAY 314: Ezekiel 22, Ezekiel 23, Psalm 145, Luke 10

☐ DAY 315: Ezekiel 24, Ezekiel 25, Psalm 146, Luke 11

☐ DAY 316: Ezekiel 26, Ezekiel 27, Proverbs 6, Luke 12

☐ DAY 317: Ezekiel 28, Ezekiel 29, Proverbs 7, Luke 13

☐ DAY 318: Ezekiel 30, Ezekiel 31, Psalm 147, Luke 14

☐ DAY 319: Ezekiel 32, Ezekiel 33, Psalm 148, Luke 15

☐ DAY 320: Ezekiel 34, Ezekiel 35, Proverbs 8, Luke 16

☐ DAY 321: Ezekiel 36, Ezekiel 37, Proverbs 9, Luke 17

☐ DAY 322: Ezekiel 38, Ezekiel 39, Psalm 149, Luke 18

☐ DAY 323: Ezekiel 40, Ezekiel 41, Psalm 150, Luke 19

☐ DAY 324: Ezekiel 42, Ezekiel 43, Proverbs 10, Luke 20

☐ DAY 325: Ezekiel 44, Ezekiel 45, Proverbs 11, Luke 21

☐ DAY 326: Ezekiel 46, Ezekiel 47, Psalm 1, Luke 22

☐ DAY 327: Ezekiel 48, Daniel 1, Proverbs 12, Luke 23

☐ DAY 328: Daniel 2, Daniel 3, Proverbs 13, Luke 24

☐ DAY 329: Daniel 4, Daniel 5, Psalm 5, John 1

☐ DAY 330: Daniel 6, Daniel 7, Proverbs 14, John 2

☐ DAY 331: Daniel 8, Daniel 9, Proverbs 15, John 3

☐ DAY 332: Daniel 10, Daniel 11, Psalm 23, John 4

☐ DAY 333: Daniel 12, Hosea 1, Proverbs 16, John 5

☐ DAY 334: Hosea 2, Hosea 3, Proverbs 17, John 6

☐ DAY 335: Hosea 4, Hosea 5, Psalm 42, John 7

☐ DAY 336: Hosea 6, Hosea 7, Proverbs 18, John 8

☐ DAY 337: Hosea 8, Hosea 9, Proverbs 19, John 9

☐ DAY 338: Hosea 10, Hosea 11, Psalm 63, John 10

☐ DAY 339: Hosea 12, Hosea 13, Hosea 14, Proverbs 20, John 11

☐ DAY 340: Joel 1, Joel 2, Proverbs 21, John 12

☐ DAY 341: Joel 3, Amos 1, Psalm 84, John 13

☐ DAY 342: Amos 2, Amos 3, Proverbs 22, John 14

☐ DAY 343: Amos 4, Amos 5, Proverbs 23, John 15

☐ DAY 344: Amos 6, Amos 7, Psalm 118, John 16

☐ DAY 345: Amos 8, Amos 9, Proverbs 24, John 17

☐ DAY 346: Obadiah 1, Jonah 1, Psalm 121, John 18

☐ DAY 347: Jonah 2, Jonah 3, Psalm 136, John 19

☐ DAY 348: Jonah 4, Micah 1, Proverbs 25, John 20

☐ DAY 349: Micah 2, Micah 3, Psalm 119:1-16, John 21

☐ DAY 350: Micah 4, Micah 5, Proverbs 26, Romans 1

☐ DAY 351: Micah 6, Micah 7, Psalm 119:17-32, Romans 2

☐ DAY 352: Nahum 1, Nahum 2, Psalm 119:33-48, Romans 3

☐ DAY 353: Nahum 3, Habakkuk 1, Proverbs 27, Romans 4

☐ DAY 354: Habakkuk 2, Habakkuk 3, Psalm 119:49-64, Romans 5

☐ DAY 355: Zephaniah 1, Zephaniah 2, Psalm 119:65-80, Romans 6

☐ DAY 356: Zephaniah 3, Haggai 1, Proverbs 28, Romans 7

☐ DAY 357: Haggai 2, Zechariah 1, Psalm 119:81-96, Romans 8

☐ DAY 358: Zechariah 2, Zechariah 3, Psalm 119:97-112, Romans 9

☐ DAY 359: Zechariah 4, Zechariah 5, Proverbs 29, Romans 10

☐ DAY 360: Zechariah 6, Zechariah 7, Psalm 119:113-128, Romans 11

☐ DAY 361: Zechariah 8, Zechariah 9, Zechariah 10, Psalm 119:129-144, Romans 12

☐ DAY 362: Zechariah 11, Zechariah 12, Proverbs 30, Romans 13

☐ DAY 363: Zechariah 13, Zechariah 14, Psalm 119:145-160, Romans 14

☐ DAY 364: Malachi 1, Malachi 2, Psalm 119:161-176, Romans 15

☐ DAY 365: Malachi 3, Malachi 4, Proverbs 31, Romans 16,

DATE

SCRIPTURE

OBSERVATION

APPLICATION

PRAYER

DATE

SCRIPTURE

OBSERVATION

APPLICATION

PRAYER

DATE

SCRIPTURE

OBSERVATION

APPLICATION

PRAYER

DATE

SCRIPTURE

OBSERVATION

APPLICATION

PRAYER

DATE

SCRIPTURE

OBSERVATION

APPLICATION

PRAYER

DATE

SCRIPTURE

OBSERVATION

APPLICATION

PRAYER

DATE

SCRIPTURE

OBSERVATION

APPLICATION

PRAYER

DATE

SCRIPTURE

OBSERVATION

APPLICATION

PRAYER

DATE

SCRIPTURE

OBSERVATION

APPLICATION

PRAYER

DATE

SCRIPTURE

OBSERVATION

APPLICATION

PRAYER

DATE

SCRIPTURE

OBSERVATION

APPLICATION

PRAYER

DATE

SCRIPTURE

OBSERVATION

APPLICATION

PRAYER

DATE

SCRIPTURE

OBSERVATION

APPLICATION

PRAYER

DATE

SCRIPTURE

OBSERVATION

APPLICATION

PRAYER

DATE

SCRIPTURE

OBSERVATION

APPLICATION

PRAYER

DATE

SCRIPTURE

OBSERVATION

APPLICATION

PRAYER

DATE

SCRIPTURE

OBSERVATION

APPLICATION

PRAYER

DATE

SCRIPTURE

OBSERVATION

APPLICATION

PRAYER

DATE

SCRIPTURE

OBSERVATION

APPLICATION

PRAYER

DATE

SCRIPTURE

OBSERVATION

APPLICATION

PRAYER

DATE

SCRIPTURE

OBSERVATION

APPLICATION

PRAYER

DATE

SCRIPTURE

OBSERVATION

APPLICATION

PRAYER

DATE

SCRIPTURE

OBSERVATION

APPLICATION

PRAYER

DATE

SCRIPTURE

OBSERVATION

APPLICATION

PRAYER

DATE

SCRIPTURE

OBSERVATION

APPLICATION

PRAYER

DATE

SCRIPTURE

OBSERVATION

APPLICATION

PRAYER

DATE

SCRIPTURE

OBSERVATION

APPLICATION

PRAYER

DATE

SCRIPTURE

OBSERVATION

APPLICATION

PRAYER

DATE

SCRIPTURE

OBSERVATION

APPLICATION

PRAYER

DATE

SCRIPTURE

OBSERVATION

APPLICATION

PRAYER

DATE

SCRIPTURE

OBSERVATION

APPLICATION

PRAYER

DATE

SCRIPTURE

OBSERVATION

APPLICATION

PRAYER

DATE

SCRIPTURE

OBSERVATION

APPLICATION

PRAYER

DATE

SCRIPTURE

OBSERVATION

APPLICATION

PRAYER

DATE

SCRIPTURE

OBSERVATION

APPLICATION

PRAYER

DATE

SCRIPTURE

OBSERVATION

APPLICATION

PRAYER

DATE

SCRIPTURE

OBSERVATION

APPLICATION

PRAYER

DATE

SCRIPTURE

OBSERVATION

APPLICATION

PRAYER

DATE

SCRIPTURE

OBSERVATION

APPLICATION

PRAYER

DATE

SCRIPTURE

OBSERVATION

APPLICATION

PRAYER

DATE

SCRIPTURE

OBSERVATION

APPLICATION

PRAYER

DATE

SCRIPTURE

OBSERVATION

APPLICATION

PRAYER

DATE

SCRIPTURE

OBSERVATION

APPLICATION

PRAYER

DATE

SCRIPTURE

OBSERVATION

APPLICATION

PRAYER

DATE

SCRIPTURE

OBSERVATION

APPLICATION

PRAYER

DATE

SCRIPTURE

OBSERVATION

APPLICATION

PRAYER

DATE

SCRIPTURE

OBSERVATION

APPLICATION

PRAYER

DATE

SCRIPTURE

OBSERVATION

APPLICATION

PRAYER

DATE

SCRIPTURE

OBSERVATION

APPLICATION

PRAYER

DATE

SCRIPTURE

OBSERVATION

APPLICATION

PRAYER

DATE

SCRIPTURE

OBSERVATION

APPLICATION

PRAYER

DATE

SCRIPTURE

OBSERVATION

APPLICATION

PRAYER

DATE

SCRIPTURE

OBSERVATION

APPLICATION

PRAYER

DATE

SCRIPTURE

OBSERVATION

APPLICATION

PRAYER

DATE

SCRIPTURE

OBSERVATION

APPLICATION

PRAYER

DATE

SCRIPTURE

OBSERVATION

APPLICATION

PRAYER

DATE

SCRIPTURE

OBSERVATION

APPLICATION

PRAYER

DATE

SCRIPTURE

OBSERVATION

APPLICATION

PRAYER

DATE

SCRIPTURE

OBSERVATION

APPLICATION

PRAYER

DATE

SCRIPTURE

OBSERVATION

APPLICATION

PRAYER

DATE

SCRIPTURE

OBSERVATION

APPLICATION

PRAYER

DATE

SCRIPTURE

OBSERVATION

APPLICATION

PRAYER

DATE

SCRIPTURE

OBSERVATION

APPLICATION

PRAYER

DATE

SCRIPTURE

OBSERVATION

APPLICATION

PRAYER

DATE

SCRIPTURE

OBSERVATION

APPLICATION

PRAYER

DATE

SCRIPTURE

OBSERVATION

APPLICATION

PRAYER

DATE

SCRIPTURE

OBSERVATION

APPLICATION

PRAYER

DATE

SCRIPTURE

OBSERVATION

APPLICATION

PRAYER

DATE

SCRIPTURE

OBSERVATION

APPLICATION

PRAYER

DATE

SCRIPTURE

OBSERVATION

APPLICATION

PRAYER

DATE

SCRIPTURE

OBSERVATION

APPLICATION

PRAYER

DATE

SCRIPTURE

OBSERVATION

APPLICATION

PRAYER

DATE

SCRIPTURE

OBSERVATION

APPLICATION

PRAYER

DATE

SCRIPTURE

OBSERVATION

APPLICATION

PRAYER

DATE

SCRIPTURE

OBSERVATION

APPLICATION

PRAYER

DATE

SCRIPTURE

OBSERVATION

APPLICATION

PRAYER

DATE

SCRIPTURE

OBSERVATION

APPLICATION

PRAYER

DATE

SCRIPTURE

OBSERVATION

APPLICATION

PRAYER

DATE

SCRIPTURE

OBSERVATION

APPLICATION

PRAYER

DATE

SCRIPTURE

OBSERVATION

APPLICATION

PRAYER

DATE

SCRIPTURE

OBSERVATION

APPLICATION

PRAYER

DATE

SCRIPTURE

OBSERVATION

APPLICATION

PRAYER

DATE

SCRIPTURE

OBSERVATION

APPLICATION

PRAYER

DATE

SCRIPTURE

OBSERVATION

APPLICATION

PRAYER

DATE

SCRIPTURE

OBSERVATION

APPLICATION

PRAYER

DATE

SCRIPTURE

OBSERVATION

APPLICATION

PRAYER

DATE

SCRIPTURE

OBSERVATION

APPLICATION

PRAYER

DATE

SCRIPTURE

OBSERVATION

APPLICATION

PRAYER

DATE

SCRIPTURE

OBSERVATION

APPLICATION

PRAYER

DATE

SCRIPTURE

OBSERVATION

APPLICATION

PRAYER

DATE

SCRIPTURE

OBSERVATION

APPLICATION

PRAYER

DATE

SCRIPTURE

OBSERVATION

APPLICATION

PRAYER

DATE

SCRIPTURE

OBSERVATION

APPLICATION

PRAYER

DATE

SCRIPTURE

OBSERVATION

APPLICATION

PRAYER

DATE

SCRIPTURE

OBSERVATION

APPLICATION

PRAYER

DATE

SCRIPTURE

OBSERVATION

APPLICATION

PRAYER

DATE

SCRIPTURE

OBSERVATION

APPLICATION

PRAYER

DATE

SCRIPTURE

OBSERVATION

APPLICATION

PRAYER

DATE

SCRIPTURE

OBSERVATION

APPLICATION

PRAYER

DATE

SCRIPTURE

OBSERVATION

APPLICATION

PRAYER

DATE

SCRIPTURE

OBSERVATION

APPLICATION

PRAYER

DATE

SCRIPTURE

OBSERVATION

APPLICATION

PRAYER

DATE

SCRIPTURE

OBSERVATION

APPLICATION

PRAYER

DATE

SCRIPTURE

OBSERVATION

APPLICATION

PRAYER

DATE

SCRIPTURE

OBSERVATION

APPLICATION

PRAYER

DATE

SCRIPTURE

OBSERVATION

APPLICATION

PRAYER

DATE

SCRIPTURE

OBSERVATION

APPLICATION

PRAYER

DATE

SCRIPTURE

OBSERVATION

APPLICATION

PRAYER

DATE

SCRIPTURE

OBSERVATION

APPLICATION

PRAYER

DATE

SCRIPTURE

OBSERVATION

APPLICATION

PRAYER

DATE

SCRIPTURE

OBSERVATION

APPLICATION

PRAYER

DATE

SCRIPTURE

OBSERVATION

APPLICATION

PRAYER

DATE

SCRIPTURE

OBSERVATION

APPLICATION

PRAYER

DATE

SCRIPTURE

OBSERVATION

APPLICATION

PRAYER

DATE

SCRIPTURE

OBSERVATION

APPLICATION

PRAYER

DATE

SCRIPTURE

OBSERVATION

APPLICATION

PRAYER

DATE

SCRIPTURE

OBSERVATION

APPLICATION

PRAYER

DATE

SCRIPTURE

OBSERVATION

APPLICATION

PRAYER

DATE

SCRIPTURE

OBSERVATION

APPLICATION

PRAYER

DATE

SCRIPTURE

OBSERVATION

APPLICATION

PRAYER

DATE

SCRIPTURE

OBSERVATION

APPLICATION

PRAYER

DATE

SCRIPTURE

OBSERVATION

APPLICATION

PRAYER

DATE

SCRIPTURE

OBSERVATION

APPLICATION

PRAYER

DATE

SCRIPTURE

OBSERVATION

APPLICATION

PRAYER

DATE

SCRIPTURE

OBSERVATION

APPLICATION

PRAYER

DATE

SCRIPTURE

OBSERVATION

APPLICATION

PRAYER

DATE

SCRIPTURE

OBSERVATION

APPLICATION

PRAYER

DATE

SCRIPTURE

OBSERVATION

APPLICATION

PRAYER

DATE

SCRIPTURE

OBSERVATION

APPLICATION

PRAYER

DATE

SCRIPTURE

OBSERVATION

APPLICATION

PRAYER

DATE

SCRIPTURE

OBSERVATION

APPLICATION

PRAYER

DATE

SCRIPTURE

OBSERVATION

APPLICATION

PRAYER

DATE

SCRIPTURE

OBSERVATION

APPLICATION

PRAYER

DATE

SCRIPTURE

OBSERVATION

APPLICATION

PRAYER

DATE

SCRIPTURE

OBSERVATION

APPLICATION

PRAYER

DATE

SCRIPTURE

OBSERVATION

APPLICATION

PRAYER

DATE

SCRIPTURE

OBSERVATION

APPLICATION

PRAYER

DATE

SCRIPTURE

OBSERVATION

APPLICATION

PRAYER

DATE

SCRIPTURE

OBSERVATION

APPLICATION

PRAYER

DATE

SCRIPTURE

OBSERVATION

APPLICATION

PRAYER

DATE

SCRIPTURE

OBSERVATION

APPLICATION

PRAYER

DATE

SCRIPTURE

OBSERVATION

APPLICATION

PRAYER

DATE

SCRIPTURE

OBSERVATION

APPLICATION

PRAYER

DATE

SCRIPTURE

OBSERVATION

APPLICATION

PRAYER

DATE

SCRIPTURE

OBSERVATION

APPLICATION

PRAYER

DATE

SCRIPTURE

OBSERVATION

APPLICATION

PRAYER

DATE

SCRIPTURE

OBSERVATION

APPLICATION

PRAYER

DATE

SCRIPTURE

OBSERVATION

APPLICATION

PRAYER

DATE

SCRIPTURE

OBSERVATION

APPLICATION

PRAYER

DATE

SCRIPTURE

OBSERVATION

APPLICATION

PRAYER

DATE

SCRIPTURE

OBSERVATION

APPLICATION

PRAYER

DATE

SCRIPTURE

OBSERVATION

APPLICATION

PRAYER

DATE

SCRIPTURE

OBSERVATION

APPLICATION

PRAYER

DATE

SCRIPTURE

OBSERVATION

APPLICATION

PRAYER

DATE

SCRIPTURE

OBSERVATION

APPLICATION

PRAYER

DATE

SCRIPTURE

OBSERVATION

APPLICATION

PRAYER

DATE

SCRIPTURE

OBSERVATION

APPLICATION

PRAYER

DATE

SCRIPTURE

OBSERVATION

APPLICATION

PRAYER

DATE

SCRIPTURE

OBSERVATION

APPLICATION

PRAYER

DATE

SCRIPTURE

OBSERVATION

APPLICATION

PRAYER

DATE

SCRIPTURE

OBSERVATION

APPLICATION

PRAYER

DATE

SCRIPTURE

OBSERVATION

APPLICATION

PRAYER

DATE

SCRIPTURE

OBSERVATION

APPLICATION

PRAYER

DATE

SCRIPTURE

OBSERVATION

APPLICATION

PRAYER

DATE

SCRIPTURE

OBSERVATION

APPLICATION

PRAYER

DATE

SCRIPTURE

OBSERVATION

APPLICATION

PRAYER

DATE

SCRIPTURE

OBSERVATION

APPLICATION

PRAYER

DATE

SCRIPTURE

OBSERVATION

APPLICATION

PRAYER

DATE

SCRIPTURE

OBSERVATION

APPLICATION

PRAYER

DATE

SCRIPTURE

OBSERVATION

APPLICATION

PRAYER

DATE

SCRIPTURE

OBSERVATION

APPLICATION

PRAYER

DATE

SCRIPTURE

OBSERVATION

APPLICATION

PRAYER

DATE

SCRIPTURE

OBSERVATION

APPLICATION

PRAYER

DATE

SCRIPTURE

OBSERVATION

APPLICATION

PRAYER

DATE

SCRIPTURE

OBSERVATION

APPLICATION

PRAYER

DATE

SCRIPTURE

OBSERVATION

APPLICATION

PRAYER

DATE

SCRIPTURE

OBSERVATION

APPLICATION

PRAYER

DATE

SCRIPTURE

OBSERVATION

APPLICATION

PRAYER

DATE

SCRIPTURE

OBSERVATION

APPLICATION

PRAYER

DATE

SCRIPTURE

OBSERVATION

APPLICATION

PRAYER

DATE

SCRIPTURE

OBSERVATION

APPLICATION

PRAYER

DATE

SCRIPTURE

OBSERVATION

APPLICATION

PRAYER

Made in the USA
Las Vegas, NV
31 October 2023

80035782R00107